*The Two Great Pillars
of Boaz and Jachin*

By Albert G. Mackey, William Harvey,
H. L. Haywood, Thomas Troward
& W. L. Fawcette

Copyright © 2020 Lamp of Trismegistus. All rights reserved. No part of this publication may be reproduced or transmitted in any form or by any means, electronic or mechanical, including photocopying, recording, or by any information storage and retrieval system, without permission in writing from Lamp of Trismegistus. Reviewers may quote brief passages.

ISBN: 978-1-63118-433-8

*Foundations of Freemasonry
Series*

Other Books in this Series and Related Titles

Masonic Symbolism of the Apron & the Altar
by Albert G. Mackey & other authors (978-1-63118-428-4)

Royal Arch, Capitular and Cryptic Masonry
by William F. Kuhn & other authors (978-1-63118-425-3)

Masonic Symbolism of Easter and the Christ in Masonry
by various authors (978-1-63118-434-5)

A Few Masonic Sermons
by A. C. Ward & Bascom B. Clarke (978-1-63118-435-2)

Masonic Symbolism of King Solomon's Temple
by Albert G. Mackey & others (978-1-63118-442-0)

Symbolism and Discourses on the Entered Apprentice, Fellowcraft and Master Mason Blue Lodge Degrees by various (978-1-63118-413-0)

The Lost Keys of Freemasonry or The Secret of Hiram Abiff
by Manly P. Hall (978-1-63118-427-7)

Plato and Platonism & Related Esoteric Essays
by H. P. Blavatsky & others (978-1-63118-432-1)

Ancient Egyptian Mysteries and Hieroglyphics, Modern Freemasonry & Initiation of the Pyramid by various (978-1-63118-430-7)

Symbolism of the Corner Stone, the North East Corner and the Religious & Masonic Symbolism of Stones by various (978-1-63118-412-3)

The Philosophy of Masonry in Five Parts by Roscoe Pound
(978-1-63118-004-0)

The Story and Legend of Hiram Abiff by William Harvey, Manly P. Hall and Albert G. Mackey (978-1-63118-411-6)

Audio Versions are also Available on Audible and iTunes

Table of Contents

Introduction...7

The Two Great Pillars
by H. L. Haywood...9

Pillars of the Porch
by Albert G. Mackey...21

Two Great Pillars
by Albert G. Mackey...35

The Dual Unity of Jachin and Boaz
by Thomas Troward...39

The History of the Two Pillars
by W. L. Fawcette...45

The Pillars of Freemasonry
by William Harvey...63

Introduction

From the beginning of Modern Freemasonry's birthdate of 1717, the intelligentsia of humanity have found refuge for safe reflection within the walls of the fraternity. Masonic writers have produced a nearly incalculable amount of written musings on a multitude of esoteric and philosophical subjects, as they relate to the ancient mysteries that Freemasonry currently storehouses. Sadly, most of it appears to have sat largely unread, as American Freemasonry in particular, continues to transform itself into something that bears little resemblance to what it was originally designed to be. The true essence of Freemasonry is not that of blind patriotism or a single-minded national religion but one of Universal Brotherhood and altruism, designed for the betterment not just of its members but of society as a whole. In particular, for those who are not members of the fraternity, as Freemasonry has always acted as a beacon, to help guide humanity through darker times, with the hopes that one day we will collectively reach a truly enlightened age.

It's not uncommon for new members joining the fraternity to find little education within the walls of many modern lodges, in spite of so much written material available to the membership. Many older members are not simply uneducated with regards to real Masonic history and symbology, not to mention the vast arena of related subjects, but they are disinterested in all of it, as well.

Lamp of Trismegistus is doing its part to help preserve humanity's Masonic history by making some of these classics available to those students who are seeking to unearth the knowledge of these ancient colossi. As such, Lamp of Trismegistus offers its readers highlights of Masonic study, culled from a variety of authors and viewpoints, with the hope bringing education back into the fraternity. So, be sure to check out other titles in our *Foundations of Freemasonry Series* as well as our *Esoteric Classics, Theosophical Classics, Occult Fiction* and our *Christian Apocrypha Series*, and don't be afraid to let a little altruism into your own heart or even into your Lodge. You can also download the audio versions of most of these titles from iTunes or Audible, for learning on the go.

The Two Great Pillars

By H. L. Haywood

I

Of all objects to which the candidate's attention is called as he begins his ascent to the Middle Chamber, none are more conspicuous, or more deserving of the most thorough investigation, than the Two Great Pillars which stand at the entrance. At one and the same time they guard the Sanctum from the outer world, and invite the Initiate into its mysteries; so noble in proportion, so intricate in design, so beautiful to see, they seem to keep solemn watch above the scene, as if to throw a hush of awe about the soul that would mount to the Upper Room of the Spirit. If throughout our history students of Masonry have surrounded them with a host of swarming theories more intricate than the network, and more multitudinous than the pomegranates it is because so many hints of ancient wisdom and secrets of symbolism have of old been hidden within these mighty columns. And if our own studies of the matter lead us to meanings numerous and almost conflicting we need not worry about it, for a symbol that says but one thing is hardly a symbol at all.

It was the custom of many of the most primitive peoples, as Frazer describes so abundantly in his "Golden Bough," to set up stones about their huts, and their villages, and over the graves of their dead. In some cases these crude rock pillars were thought to be the abodes of gods or demons;

in others, homes of the ghosts; and often as symbols of sex. Of the last-named usage one writer has said that "pillars of stone, when associated with worship, have been from time immemorial regarded as symbols of the active and passive, the generative and fecundating principles." In Egypt, Horus and Sut were regarded as two living pillars, twin builders and supporters of the heavens, and Sir Arthur Evans has shown that pillars "were everywhere worshipped as gods." "In India, and among the Mayas and Incas," we read in "The Builders," "there were three pillars at the portals of the earthly and skyey temple—Wisdom, Strength, and Beauty. When man set up a pillar, he became a fellow worker with Him whom the old sages of China used to call the first Builder. Also, pillars were set up to mark the holy places of vision and Divine deliverance, as when Jacob erected a pillar at Bethel, Joshua at Gilgal, and Samuel at Mizpeh and Shen. Always they were symbols of stability, of what the Egyptians described as 'the place of establishing forever'—emblem of the faith 'that the pillars of the earth are the Lords,' and He hath set the world upon them."

"In all countries," remarks another writer, "as the earliest of man's work we recognize the sublime, mysteriously speaking, ever recurring monolith": but by no people were pillars so venerated, or so variously used as by the Egyptians. Originally, perhaps, they served as astronomical instruments to mark the time, to denote the stages of the heavenly bodies, and to assist in the orienting of temples. Connected with the places of worship they were gradually associated with the gods, and became in time symbols of deity, as we may learn from Professor Breasted's "History of the Development of Religion and Thought in Ancient Egypt," in which delightful book he tells us that the obelisk, as Egyptians called the pillar, came at last to stand pre-eminently for the great Sun God.

This veneration of upstanding stones answered so deep a need in man's habits of worship that it proved to be one of the last forms of idolatry to give way before Monotheism, the worship of the One Invisible God. The Israelites, as the Bible witnesses, cling stubbornly to their "stocks and stones," reverence for which they may have learned in Egypt during their long sojourn there; and even in Christian countries the custom remained with such tenacity that the Lateran Council formally prohibited stone worship as late at 452.

From Egypt, it is said, the custom of placing Pillars before temples was borrowed by the Phoenicians, but this has been somewhat disputed; be that as it may, we know that Hiram of Tyre erected two great columns before his magnificent temple of Melkarth, where Herodotus saw them five centuries afterwards. It was these, perhaps, that served Hiram as models for the more famous Pillars which he erected before the Temple of Solomon.

Of these Pillars one description is in the Book of Kings, another in the Book of Chronicles. In the former record the height is given as eighteen cubits; in the latter as thirty-five; if a cubit be accepted as denoting eighteen inches, the former height would be twenty-seven, the latter fifty-two and one-half feet, a variation of twenty-five feet. To explain this discrepancy scholars have supposed Kings to give the height of only one, Chronicles the combined height of both, leaving allowances for the sockets of the head-pieces. Concerning these head-pieces, historians have differed, but none have given a clearer explanation than Mackey:

"Above the pillar, and covering its upper part to the depth of nine inches, was an oval body or chapiter seven feet and a half in height. Springing out from the pillar, at the junction of the chapiter with it, was a row of lotus petals, which, first spreading around the chapiter, afterwards gently curved downward towards the pillar, something like the Acanthus leaves on the capital of a Corinthian column. About two-fifths of the distance from the bottom of the chapiter, or just below its most bulging part, a tissue of network was carved, which extended over its whole upper surface. To the bottom of this network was suspended a series of fringes, and on these again were carved two rows of pomegranates, one hundred being in each row."

II

The Pillars were cylindrical in shape, probably, and were cast of brass, and the combined weight must have been not less than fifty-three tons. One of them was called Boaz, the other Jachin, and the former stood in the northeast corner of the Porch, the latter in the southeast; Jachin was the right pillar, Boaz the left, and this means that right and left have reference to one standing inside the Temple, which faced the East. According to the tradition, the Pillars were cast in foundries situated between Succoth and Zeredatha, about thirty-five miles northeast of Jerusalem, whose moulders and jewellers still use clay brought from that region.

The network about the chapiter was probably an ornamental lattice work of metal, though some think it was an interlacing of branches or vines. The lily-work, doubtless, was a formal design, made to represent a species of the Egyptian lotus, a sacred plant among the dwellers of the Nile and much used by them. There were no globes on these Pillars, though the chapiters themselves were spherical; the globes were added at a late date by some Masonic ritualist, Preston it may be.

Those Pillars, strange to say, were not often copied by mediæval builders, though they seem to have been imitated in the Cathedral of Notre Dame, at Poitiers, erected in 1161; and in the Wurtzburg Cathedral, in Bavaria, the work, it seems, of the Comacines. But at a very early date they were used by Masons for symbolical purposes, as testified by the history of the Compagnonage, and by the "Old Charges" of the Freemasons.

In the latter we find a curious legend. The Cooke MS. of about 1350 relates that before Noah's flood, Jabal, Jubal, and Tubal Cain knew that God was to destroy the world; "wherefore they wrote the sciences that they had found out on two pillars of stone. Hermes, that was son to Cush, afterwards found the two pillars, and the sciences written thereon; and Abraham taught them to the Egyptians." Inasmuch as it was supposed that Masonry had come from Egypt the old chronicles thus quaintly sought to link their traditions up to the very beginnings of the world. From these Old Charges, we may suppose, the legend crept into the symbolic lore of the Craft, and was thus preserved until Speculative days, when the Pillar symbolism became embodied in the Rituals as we now have them.

It has often been shown that in the descriptions and interpretations given in our work of the Pillars there are many inaccuracies and inconsistencies. Thus, only fourteen American jurisdictions use the Pillars as being eighteen cubits in height; one jurisdiction makes them thirty, and twenty-seven make them thirty-five! Thirty-five cubits is a lofty height indeed and would make the Pillars entirely out of proportion to a Temple that was only ninety feet long and thirty feet wide! But such inaccuracies as these, historical and architectural, need not trouble us if we will but keep in mind the fact that with us the Pillars have become symbols of truth, and that errors of fact do not touch the hidden meanings.

What are these hidden meanings? William Preston saw in them a reference to the Pillar of Cloud and the Pillar of Fire by which, it is said, the Israelites were guided, and accordingly made them to stand for Providence. This is ingenious but altogether out of harmony with the long historical use of the emblems, for no other interpreter had ever found such meanings in them. Caldecott believed that the Jewish king stood before one Pillar in public ceremonies and the High Priest before the other, and that the Pillars consequently stand for Government and Religion in society. Brother Covey-Crump, writing in the *Transactions of the Authors' Lodge*, vol. I, made them to stand for Space and Time, the two pillars through which the human mind passes into knowledge; of similar character is the other reading which sees in them the two tropics of Cancer and Capricorn. Mackey, reasoning from their names, Jachin, which means, "He shall establish," and Boaz, "In it is strength," makes them to mean the strength and the stability of Masonry.

Many of the old Jewish Rabbis, afterwards followed by the Kabbalists, found in them the symbolism of birth; as one wrote: "The names of the pillars signified potency and perpetuity; the pomegranates on their capitals or chapiters were symbols of generation." With this, after everything is taken into consideration, I am inclined to agree. Being properly stationed at the door of the lodge room, or on the Porch of the Temple, they signify entrance, for it is through them that the candidate passes to his initiation, and Initiation, as we have already seen, is birth into a new life.

When thus understood the Two Pillars represent a law that applies throughout the world of men, as well as in the lodge, and that in a sense not at all far-fetched. We have learned that many of our human ills spring from bad heredity and come to us in birth, and not until men are well born will they be well men, sound in body and soul. And what is true of birth into life is also true of any new birth into any of the realms of life. If the pillars at the door of the family be strong and clean the child will be wholesome and happy in its life therein. If wise men guard the doorways of the schools our youth will enter into the mind's world of light and power, but not otherwise. For always is it, that if one would anywhere become a Master he must make a right entrance into Life's Temple. And he who thus lives will himself become a Pillar, strengthened and strengthening, against which Kings and Priests may lean, and past which others may be enabled to enter into the life that is life indeed. Woe be it to human society, if ever it neglects to give, in any of its spheres, right birth to its children, its seekers and learners!

III

On the top of each of the Two Pillars thus described stand two Globes, one, the Celestial, representing the heavens; the other, the Terrestrial, representing the earth. Whence came these? and what do they signify?

In answer to the first of these questions our scholars have offered two hypotheses: first, that they are of Egyptian origin; second, that they are a modified form of the chapiters, or head-pieces, of the Two Pillars. The first of these theories was evidently suggested by the ancient Egyptian symbol of the winged globe, often found on the entablature above a temple surrounded by a snake holding its tail in its mouth and flanked by two wide, outstretched wings. So common was this device that it became at last one of the national emblems, so that Isaiah speaks of Egypt as "the land of the winged globe." This globe was in all probability oval in shape, to suggest the egg, symbol of life; the serpent was the symbol of infinity; the wings, of power; combined, the figure stood for the infinite life-giving power of Deity. If it be supposed that the globe was a true circle, as some contend that it was, instead of an oval then it may have represented the Sun, the first great god of Egypt, but the meaning remains practically the same.

If our two Globes could be made to serve as a modern form of the Egyptian winged globe they might be enriched in meaning and interest, but there is no evidence whatever that the older symbol ever transmigrated into Masonry. The probability is all against it, for we have two globes instead of one, and we do not have the serpent or the wings; besides, as actually exhibited, our Globes manifestly refer to the earth and the heavens as modernly understood.

The chapiters on the Two Pillars were spherical in shape and always so represented. It would evidently seem, therefore, that the men who framed our present Ritual of the Second Step, among whom Preston was conspicuous, simply modified the chapiters into Globes. But why did they do this? Because Preston and his circle undertook to transform the lodge into a school and consequently required symbols for geography and astronomy, two very important branches of the curriculum they outlined. This theory is verified, it seems to me, by reference to the Prestonian lectures, in which we find the following paragraphs, as slightly abridged by Webb:

"The sphere, with the parts of the earth delineated on its surface, is called the Terrestrial Globe; and that with the constellations, and other heavenly bodies, the Celestial Globe.

"The principal use of the Globes, besides serving as maps to distinguish the outward parts of the earth, and the situation of the fixed stars, is to illustrate and explain the phenomena arising from the annual revolution and the diurnal rotation of the earth around its own axis. *They are the noblest instruments for improving the mind* [this was Preston's motive—H.L.H.], and giving it the most distinct idea of any problem or proposition, as well as enabling it to solve the same."

Some of our writers have ridiculed all this. They say that the use now made of the globes is schoolboyish. Perhaps! but even so, the idea behind it all is sound and worthy of serious consideration. It is good to think about this marvelous planet on which we live, and it is good to gaze into the heavens by which we are surrounded. The heavens and the earth together, this is the Universe, the All-Thing as the old Norsemen called it, the contemplation of which, as old Samuel Kant once confessed, fills one with unspeakable awe. If a man cannot feel reverence in the presence of all that which is represented by the Two Globes there is something lacking out of his nature.

Pillars of the Porch

By Albert G. Mackey

The pillars most remarkable in Scripture history were the two erected by Solomon at the porch of the Temple, and which Josephus (Antiquities of the Jews, Book I, chapter ii) thus describes: "Moreover, this Hiram made two hollow pillars, whose outsides were of brass, and the thickness of the brass was four fingers' breadth, and the height of the pillars was eighteen cubits, or twenty-seven feet, and the circumference, twelve cubits, or eighteen feet; but there was cast with each of their chapiters lily-work, that stood upon the pillar, and it was elevated five cubits, seven and a half feet, round about which there was net-work interwoven with small palms made of brass, and covered the lily-work. To this also were hung two hundred pomegranates, in two rows. The one of these pillars he set at the entrance of the porch on the right hand, or South, and called it Jachin, and the other at the left hand, or North, and called it Boaz."

It has been supposed that Solomon, in erecting these pillars, had reference to the pillar of cloud and the pillar of fire which went before the Israelites in the wilderness, and that the right hand or South pillar represented the pillar of cloud, and the left hand or North pillar represented that of fire. Solomon did not simply erect them as ornaments to the Temple, but as memorials of God's repeated promises of support to his people of Israel. For the pillar Jachin, derived from the words Jah, meaning Jehovah, and achin, to establish, signifies that God will establish His house of Israel; while the pillar Boas, compounded of b, meaning in and oaz, strength, signifies that in strength skull it be established.

And thus were the Jews in passing through the porch to the Temple, daily reminded of the abundant promises of God, and inspired with confidence in his protection and gratitude for his many acts of kindness to his chosen people.

There is no part of the architecture of the ancient Temple which is so difficult to be understood in its details as the scriptural account of these memorable pillars. Freemasons, in general, intimately as their symbolical signification is connected with some of the most beautiful portions of their ritual, appear to have but a confused notion of their construction and of the true disposition of the various parts of which they are composed. Ferguson says that there are no features connected with the Temple which have given rise to so much controversy, or been so difficult to explain, as the form of these two pillars.

Their situation, according to Lightfoot, was within the porch, at its very entrance, and on each side of the gate. They were therefore seen, one on the right and the other on the left, AS soon as the visitor stepped within the porch. And this, it will be remembered, in confirmation, is the very spot in which Ezekiel (xi, 49), places the pillars that he saw in his vision of the Temple. "The length of the porch was twenty cubits, and the breadth eleven cubits; and he brought me by the steps whereby they went up to it, and there were pillars by the posts, one on this side, and another on that side." The assertion made by some writers, that they were not columns intended to support the roof, but simply obelisks for ornament, is not sustained by sufficient authority; and as Ferguson very justly says, not only would the high roof look painfully weak, but it would have been impossible to construct it, with the imperfect science of those days, without some such support. These pillars, we are told, were of brass, as well as the chapiters that surmounted them, and were cast hollow. The thickness of the brass of each pillar was "four fingers, or a hand's breadth," which is equal to three inches. According to the amounts in *First Kings*, and in *Jeremiah*, the circumference of each pillar was twelve cubits. Now, according to the Jewish computation, the cubit used in the measurement of the Temple buildings was six hands' breadth, or eighteen inches. recording to the tables of Bishop Cumberland, the cubit was rather more, he making it about twenty-two inches; but Brother Mackey adheres to the measure laid down by the Jewish writers as probably more correct, and certainly more simple for calculation. The circumference of each pillar, reduced by this scale to English measure, would be eighteen feet, and its diameter about six.

The reader of the scriptural accounts of these pillars will be not a little puzzled with the apparent discrepancies that are found in the estimates of their height as given in the *Books of Kings* and *Chronicles*. In the former book, it is said that their height was eighteen cubits, and in the latter it was thirty-five, which latter height Whiston observes would be contrary to all the rules of architecture. But the discrepancy is easily reconciled by supposing—which, indeed, must have been the case that in the *Book of Kings* the pillars are spoken of separately, and that in *Chronicles* their aggregate height is calculated; and the reason why, in this latter book, their united height is placed at thirty-five cubits instead of thirty-six, which would be the double of eighteen, is because they are there measured as they appeared with the chapters upon them. Now half a cubit of each pillar was concealed in what Lightfoot calls "the whole of the chapiter," that is, half a cubit's depth of the lower edge of the chapiter covered the top of the pillar, making each pillar, apparently, only seventeen and a half cubits high, or the two thirty-five cubits as laid down in the *Book of Chronicles*.

This is a much better method of reconciling the discrepancy than that adopted by Calcott, who supposes that the pedestals of the pillars were seventeen cubits high—a violation of every rule of architectural proportion with which we would be reluctant to charge the memory of so "cunning a workman" as Hiram the Builder. The account in *Jeremiah* agrees with that in the Book of Rings. The height, therefore, of each of these pillars was, in English measure, twenty-seven feet. The chapiter or pommel was five cubits, or seven and a half feet more; but as half a cubit, or nine inches, was common to both pillar and chapiter, the whole height from the ground to the top of the chapiter was twenty-two cubits and a half, or thirty-three feet and nine inches.

Ferguson has come to a different conclusion. He save in the article Temple, in *Smith's Dictionary of the Bible*, that "according to *First Kings*, the pillars were eighteen cubits high and twelve in circumference, with capitals five cubits in height. Above this was another member, called also chapter of lily-work, four cubits in height, but which, from the second mention of it in verse 22, seems more probably to have been an entablature, which is necessary to complete the order. As these members make out twenty-seven cubits, leaving three cubits, or four and a half feet, for the slope of the roof, the whole design seems reasonable and proper." He calculates, of course, on the authority of the *Book of Kings*, that the height of the roof of the porch was thirty cubits, and assumes that these pillars were columns by which it was supported, and connected with it by an entablature.

Each of these pillars was surmounted by a chapiter, which was five cubits, or seven and a half feet in height. The shape and construction of this chapiter require some consideration. The Hebrew word which is used in this place is koteret. Its root is to be found in the word keter, which signified a crown, and is so used in *Esther*, to designate the Royal diadem of the King of Persia. The Chaldaic version expressly calls the chapiter a crown; but Rabbi Solomon, in his Commentary, uses the word ponel, signifying a globe or spherical body, and Rabbi Gershom describes it as "like two crowns joined together." Lightfoot says, "it was a huge, great oval, five cubits high, and did not only sit upon the head of the pillars, but also flowered or spread them, being larger about, a great deal, than the pillars themselves." The Jewish commentators say that the two lower cubits of its surface were entirely plain, but that the three upper were richly ornamented.

In the *First Book of Kings*, the ornaments of the chapiters are thus described:

And nets of checker-work and wreaths of chain-work for the chapiters which were upon the tops of the pillars seven for the one chapiter, and seven for the other chapiter And he made the pillars, and two rows round about upon the one net-work, to cover the chapiters that were upon the top, with pomegranates; and so did he for the other chapiter. And the chapiters that were upon the top of the pillars were of lily-work in the porch, four cubits.

And the chapiters upon the two pillars had pomegranates also above, over against the belly, which was by the net-work; and the pomegranates were two hundred in rows, round about upon the other chapiter.

And upon the top of the pillars was lily-work- so was the work of the pillars finished. Let us endeavor to render this description, which does appear somewhat confused and unintelligible, plainer and more comprehensible.

The "nets of checker-work" is the first ornament mentioned. The words thus translated are in the original which Lightfoot prefers rendering thickets of branch work; and he thinks that the true meaning of the passage is that "the chapiters were curiously wrought with branch work, seven goodly branches standing up from the belly of the oval, and their boughs and leaves curiously and lovely intermingled and interwoven one with another." He derives his reason for this version from the fact that the same word, is translated thicket in the passage in *Genesis*, where the ram is described as being "caught in a thicket by his horns"; and in various other passages the word is to be similarly translated.

But, on the other hand, we find it used in the *Book of Job*, where it evidently signifies a net made of meshes: "For he is cast into a net by his own feet and he walketh upon a snare." In *Second Kings*, the same word is used, where our translators have rendered it a lattice; "Ahaziah fell down through a lattice in his upper chamber." Brother Mackey was, therefore, not inclined to adopt the emendation of Lightfoot, but rather coincide with the received version, as well as the Masonic tradition, that this ornament was a simple network or fabric consisting of reticulated lines—in other words, a lattice-work.

The "wreaths of chain-work" that are next spoken of are less difficult to be understood. The word here translated Wreath is and is to be found in *Deuteronomy*, where it distinctly mean syringes: "Thou shalt make thee fringes upon the four quarters of thy vesture." Fringes it should also be translated here. "The fringes of chain-work," Doctor Mackey thought, were therefore attached to, and hung down from, the network spoken of above, and were probably in this case, as when used upon the garments of the Jewish High Priests, intended as a "memorial of the law."

The "lily-work" is the last ornament that demands our attention. And here the description of Lightfoot is so clear and evidently correct, that Doctor Mackey did not hesitate to quote it at length. "At the head of the pillar, even at the setting on of the chaptiter, there was a curious and a large border or circle of lily-work, which stood out four cubits under the chapiter, and then turned down, every lily or lona tongue of brass, with a neat bending. and so seemed as a flowered crown to the head of the pillar, and as a curious garland whereon the chapiter had its seat."

There is a very common error among Freemasons, which has been fostered by the plates in our Monitors, hat there were on the pillars chapiters, and that these chapiters were again surmounted by globes. The truth, however, is that the chapiters themselves rere "the pommels or globes," to which our lecture, in the Fellow Crafty Degree, alludes. This is evident from what has already been said in the first art of the preceding description. The lily here spoken of is not at all related, as might be supposed, to the common lily—that one spoken of in the New Testament- It was a species of the lotus, the Symnhaea lotos, or lotus of the Nile. This was among the Egyptians a sacred plant, found everywhere on their monuments, and used in their architectural decorations. It is evident, from their descriptions, that the pillars of the porch of King Solomon's Temple were copied from the pillars of the Egyptian Temples. The maps of the earth and the charts of the celestial constellations which are sometimes said to have been engraved upon these globes, must be referred to the pillars, where, according to Doctor Oliver, a Masonic tradition places them— an ancient custom, instances of which we find in profane history. this is, however, by no means of any importance, as the symbolic allusion is perfectly well preserved in the shapes of the chapiters, without the necessity of any such geographical or astronomical engraving upon them. For being globular, or nearly so, they may be justly said to have represented the celestial and terrestrial spheres.

The true description, then, of these memorable pillars, is simply this: Immediately within the porch of the Temple, and on each side of the door, were placed two hollow brazen pillars. The height of each was twenty-seven feet, the diameter about six feet, and the thickness of the brass three inches. Above the pillar, and covering its upper part to the depth of nine inches, was an oval body or chapiter seven feet and a half in height. Springing out from the pillar, at the junction of the chapiter with it, was a row of lotus petals, which, first spreading around the chapiter, afterward gently curved downward toward the pillar, something like the Acanthus leaves on the capital of a Corinthian column.

About two-fifths of the distance from the bottom of the chapiter, or just below its most bulging part, a tissue of network was carved, which extended over its whole upper surface. To the bottom of this network was suspended a series of fringes, and on these again were carved two rows of pomegranates, one hundred being in each row. This description, it seemed to Doctor Mackey, is the only one that can be reconciled with the various passages in the *Books of Kings*, *Chronicles*, and *Josephus*, which relate to these pillars, and the only one that can give the Masonic student a correct conception of the architecture of these important symbols.

And now as to the Masonic symbolism of these two pillars. As symbols they have been very universally diffused and are to be found in all rites. Nor are they of a very recent date, for they are depicted on the earliest tracing-boards, and are alluded to in the catechisms before the middle of the eighteenth century. Nor is this surprising; for as the symbolism of Freemasonry is founded on the Temple of Solomon, it was to be expected that these important parts of the Temple would be naturally included in the system. But at first the pillars appear to have been introduced into the lectures rather as parts of a historical detail than as significant symbols—an idea which seems gradually to have grown up. The catechism of 1731 describes their name, their size, and their material, but says nothing of their symbolic import. Yet this had been alluded to in the Scriptural account of them, which says that the names bestowed upon them were significant. What was the original or Scriptural symbolism of the pillars has been very well explained by Dudley, in his Naology. He says:

> The pillars represented the sustaining power of the great God. The flower of the lotus of water-lily rises from a root growing at the bottom of the water, and maintains its position on the surface by its columnar stalk, which becomes more or less straight as occasion requires; it is therefore aptly symbolical of the power of the Almighty constantly employed to secure the safety of all the world. The chapiter is the body or mass of the earth; the pomegranates, fruits remarkable for the number of their seeds, are symbols of fertility; the wreaths drawn variously over the surface of the chapiter or globe indicate the courses of the heavenly bodies in the heavens around the earth,

and the variety of the seasons. The pillars were properly placed in the porch or portico of the Temple, for they suggested just ideas of the power of the Almighty, of the entire dependence of man upon him, the Creator; and doing this, they exhorted all to fear, to love, and obey Him.

It was, however, Hutchinson who first introduced the symbolic idea of the pillars into the Masonic system. He says:

The pillars erected at the porch of the Temple were not only ornamental. but also carried with them an emblematical import in their names: Boaz being, in its literal translation. in thee is strength; and Jachin, it shad be established, which, by a very natural transposition, may be put thus: O Lord, Thou art mighty, and Thy power is established from everlasting to everlasting.

Preston subsequently introduced the symbolism, considerably enlarged, into his system of lectures. He adopted the reference to the pillars of fire and cloud, which is still retained. The Masonic symbolism of the two pillars may be considered, without going into minute details, as being twofold. First, in reference to the names of the pillars, they are symbols of the strength and stability of the Institution; and then in reference to the ancient pillars of fire and cloud, they are symbolic of our dependence on the superintending guidance of the Great Architect of the Universe, by which around that strength and stability are secured.

The foregoing article by Doctor Mackey may well be supplemented here by such later information as is, for example, contained in Hasting's Dictionary of the Bible. From this later authority we find that the hollow pillars had a thickness of metal equal to three inches of our measure. Their height on the basis of the larger cubit of twenty and one-half inches was about thirty-one feet, while their diameter works out at about six and one-half feet. The capitals appear from *First Kings*, to have been globes or of some such shape, each about eight and one-half feet in height, giving a total height for the complete pillars of, roughly, forty feet. They may be regarded as structurally independent of the Temple Porch and stood free in front of it, Jachin on the south and Boaz on the north, one on either side of the steps leading up to the entrance of the Porch.

Such free-standing pillars were a feature of the Phoenician and other Temples of Western Asia. The names Jachin and Boaz are not now translated with the same assurance as formerly. Various meanings have been assigned and one of the more suggestive explanations is that they refer to Baal and Jachun, the latter being a Phoenician verbal form of the same signification—He wig be—as the Hebrew Jahweh, both words having been used as synonyms for Deity.

The fact that the pillars were the work of the Tyrian artist makes it probable that their presence is to be explained with the analogy in mind of similar pillars of Phoenician Temples. These, though they were viewed in primitive times as the dwelling-place of the Deity, had, as civilization and religion advanced, come to be regarded as merely symbols of His sacred presence. To a Phoenician Temple architect such as Hiram Abiff, Jachin and Boaz would appear as natural additions to such a religious structure and are, therefore, as Kennedy suggests, perhaps best explained as conventional symbols of God for whose worship the Temple of Solomon was designed and built.

Two Great Pillars

By Albert G. Mackey

The oldest existing Tracing Boards of early Eighteenth Century Lodges contain the two Pillars. One gathers from the Minutes that during the days when Lodges had their dining table in the center of the Lodge room and sat around it while a Candidate was being initiated, the Tracing Board, painted on cloth, was laid on the floor, or hung on the wall, and "lectures" were used to explain it. The set of symbols in the still-existing Tracing Boards correspond 80 closely to those mentioned in the Legend of the Craft in the Old Charges that it is reasonable to believe that the key to the interpretation of the symbols given to the Candidate is found in the latter. If that be true, the two pillars in the Tracing Boards in the oldest of the Lodges must have referred to the two pillars described in the Cooke MS., one of marble and one of "lacerns," or tile.

When the Allegory of Solomon's Temple was introduced into the Second Degree, perhaps about 1740 or 1750 in its present form, the two Great Pillars belonging to it came into a prominent place. This meant that the older Lodges then had two sets of Pillars. Whether the former was dropped out, or the two became coalesced, it is impossible to know.

In some of the Tracing Boards and in engravings used on certificates, etc., three pillars often were used, but these probably represented columns; and in some instances these were either Wisdom, Strength, and Beauty, or else, to judge by the figures sometimes shown on top of them, the three Theological Virtues of Faith, Hope, and Charity. With the columns representing the Five Orders, Lodge symbolism contained no fewer than ten, and it may even have been thirteen, pillars and columns together.

Two problems about the Temple pillars are not yet solved: first, whether they stood out on the platform beyond the Temple, or stood in the facade of it, and as structural members of the building; second, what their height was. The narrative in the Book of Kings does not give an answer to either question. On the basis of the general custom in Egypt and in the Near East it is most likely that the Two Pillars stood apart from the building; and it is possible that the Chapters on their tops were really large metal baskets which could be filled with burning pine or cedar knots for illumination at night, and also possibly as a reminiscence of the pillar of cloud by day and of fire by night.

There were four cubits, or units of measurement, in use. Generally, a cubit was the distance from the elbow to the end of the fingers, but the others differed; in one instance, one of the cubits in use is almost twice the length of another. The Book of Kings does not say which cubit was employed, but if the Pillars were in the facade of the building and formed two sides of the entrance they were probably about seventeen feet high; if, as is more likely, they stood apart they were probably thirty-four feet high. As far as known records go the early Speculative Masons saw so little of importance in the question of height that apparently they never decided it one way or another; in any event, the exact height means nothing to the symbolism.

In both the oldest Minutes and the oldest engravings the two Globes appear to have been unconnected with the Pillars. They were put sometimes in one place in the room and sometimes in another. Remarks incorporated here and there in the Minutes suggest that the Brethren used them to represent "the universality of Masonry," not in the sense that Masonry took in everything but in the sense that Lodges are constituted in every country. One globe was the sky, the other the land; together they made up the world. The two Great Pillars in the Old Charges represented the Liberal Arts and Sciences; in the Allegory of Solomon's Temple they were guardians and gates to the Presence of Jehovah; both of these interpretations became loosely fused in the Second Degree.

By a similar development of symbolic interpretation the Terrestrial Globe came also to mean the earth, the earthy; the Celestial, to mean the heavenly, the spiritual. When the Globes and the Pillars were combined both sets of symbolism were synthesized, so that as used in modern Speculative Rituals they are very rich in significance, not the least of which was the complete fusing of education (Seven Liberal Arts and Sciences) with religion (Temple worship), an idea in absolute contrast to the Medieval idea, when church and school were often at war with each other, and faith and knowledge were considered to be opposites, or foes.

The Dual Unity of Jachin and Boaz

By Thomas Troward

"And he reared up the pillars before the temple, one on the right hand, and the other on the left; and called the name of that on the right hand Jachin, and the name of that on the left Boaz." (II Chron. iii, 17.)

Very likely some of us have wondered what was the meaning of these two mysterious pillars set up by Solomon in front of his temple, and why they were called by these strange names; and then we have dropped the subject as one of those inexplicable things handed down in the Bible from old time which, we suppose, can have no practical interest for us at the present day. Nevertheless, these strange names are not without a purpose. They contain the key to the entire Bible and to the whole order of Nature, and as emblems of the two great principles that are the pillars of the universe, they fitly stood at the threshold of that temple which was designed to symbolize all the mysteries of Being.

In all the languages of the Semitic stock the letters J and Y are interchangeable, as we see in the modern Arabic "Yakub" for "Jacob" and the old Hebrew "Yaveh" for "Jehovah." This gives us the form "Yachin," which at once reveals the enigma. The word Yak signifies "one"; and the termination "h-i," or "h-i-n," is an intensitive which may be rendered in English by the word "only." Thus the word "Yakin" or "Jachin" resolves itself into the words "one only," meaning: the all-embracing Unity.

The meaning of Boaz is clearly seen in the book of Ruth. There Boaz appears as the kinsman exercising the right of pre-emption so familiar to those versed in Oriental law--a right which has for its purpose the maintenance of the Family as the social unit. According to this widely-spread custom, the purchaser, who is not a member of the family, buys the property subject to the right of kinsmen within certain degrees to purchase it back, and so bring it once more into the family to which it originally belonged. Whatever may be our personal opinions regarding the vexed questions of dogmatic theology, we can all agree as to the general principle indicated in the role acted by Boaz. He brings back the alienated estate into the family--that is to say, he "redeems" it in the legal sense of the word. As a matter of law his power to do this, results from his membership in the family; but his motive for doing it is love, his affection for Ruth. Without pushing the analogy too far we may say, then, that Boaz represents the principle of redemption in the widest sense of reclaiming an estate by right of relationship, while the innermost moving power in its recovery is Love.

This is what Boaz stands for in the beautiful story of Ruth, and there is no reason why we should not let the same name stand for the same thing when we seek the meaning of the mysterious pillar. Thus the two pillars typify Unity and the redeeming power of Love, with the significant suggestion that the redemption results from the Unity. They correspond with the two "bonds," or uniting principles spoken of by St. Paul, "the Unity of the Spirit which is the Bond of Peace," and "Love, which is the Bond of Perfectness."

The former is Unity of Being; the latter, Unity of Intention: and the principle of this Dual-Unity is well illustrated by the story of Boaz. The whole story proceeds on the idea of the Family as the social unit, the root-conception of all Oriental law, and if we consider the Family in this light, we shall see how exactly it embodies the two-fold idea of Jachin and Boaz, unity of Being and unity of Thought. The Family forms a unit because all the members proceed from a common progenitor, and are thus all of one blood; but, although this gives them a natural unity of Being of which they cannot divest themselves, it is not enough in itself to make them a united family, as unfortunately experience too often shows. Something more is wanted, and that something is Love. There must be a personal union brought about by sympathetic Thought to complete the natural union resulting from birth. The inherent unity must be expressed by the Individual volition of each member, and thus the Family becomes the ideally perfect social unit; a truth to which St. Paul alludes when he calls God the Father from Whom every family in heaven and on earth is named. Thus Boaz stands for the principle which brings back to the original Unity that which has been for a time separated from it. There has never been any separation of actual Being--the family right always subsisted in the property even while in the hands of strangers, otherwise it could never have been brought back; but it requires the Love principle to put this right into effective operation.

When this begins to work in the knowledge of its right to do so, then there is the return of the individual to the Unity, and the recognition of himself as the particular expression of the Universal in virtue of his own nature.

These two pillars, therefore, stand for the two great spiritual principles that are the basis of all Life: Jachin typifying the Unity resulting from Being, and Boaz typifying the Unity resulting from Love. In this Dual-Unity we find the key to all conceivable involution or evolution of Spirit; and it is therefore not without reason that the record of these two ancient pillars has been preserved in our Scriptures. And finally we may take this as an index to the character of our Scriptures generally. They contain infinite meanings; and often those passages which appear on the surface to be most meaningless will be found to possess the deepest significance. The Book, which we often read so superficially, hides beneath its sometimes seemingly trivial words the secrets of other things. The twin pillars Jachin and Boaz bear witness to this truth.

-oOo-

The *Two Pillars* of the Universe are Personality and Mathematics, represented by Boaz and Jachin respectively. This is the broadest simplification to which it is possible to reduce things. Balance consists in preserving the Equilibrium or Alternating Current between these two Principles. Personality is the Absolute Factor. Mathematics are the Relative Factor, for they merely Measure different Rates or Scales. They are absolute in this respect. A particular scale having been selected all its sequences will follow by an inexorable Law of Order and Proportion; but the selection of the scale and the change from one scale to another, rests entirely with Personality. What Personality can not do is to make one Scale produce the results of another, but it can set aside one scale and substitute another for it. Hence Personality contains in itself the Universal Scale, or can either accommodate itself to lower rates of motion already established, or can raise them to its own rate of motion. Hence Personality is the grand Ultimate Fact in all things.

Different personalities should be regarded as different degrees of consciousness. They are different degrees of emergence of The Power that knows Itself.

The History of the Two Pillars

By W. L. Fawcette

The interest in relics has its foundation in the transitory nature of all material forms and the difficulty with which man makes any permanent impression upon them. It has taken but a thousand years or so to obliterate the monumental evidences of some of the greatest cities of the world. A few manuscript books have lasted a little longer, but time at last tyrannizes over all; walls crumble, the ancient books go piecemeal to rags, languages die, the meaning of words and symbols changes, and it requires the continuous attention of man to rescue anything from the sea of oblivion that continually encroaches upon the shores of history. A few leading ideas and words seem to last forever, but, as a rule, all human handiwork that appeals to the eye disappears sooner or later; and when we meet with any artificial object which presents to our eyes a form preserved while cities have crumbled and nations have vanished, it seems a new revelation of the past. But it is in the unexpected discovery that familiar words, ideas, and objects have a pedigree as long as chronology itself, that we get, perhaps, the most vivid impression of contact with the past, and that shadowy hands seem to reach out suddenly from some mysterious storehouse of dead and dusty things to clasp our own. For the great majority of even educated people, such an experience as this may be found in the history of the modern dollar-mark, $. How little does the clerk, shopkeeper, or banker who makes a hundred times a day this familiar figure, imagine he is making representations of the oldest symbol known to the human race; one which seems to have been elaborated out of the mythologies of all the ancients, passing through numberless changes by the outgrowth of fanciful legends from the original ideas, but clearly traceable to the earliest races, of whom we get only shadowy outlines in the dusk of antiquity, — a symbol known to those who built Tyre and Carthage as "the pillars of Heracles," but as ancient to them as to us. In comparatively modern times poetic fancy has conferred this name on the two mountains that stand at the entrance to the Mediterranean,— Calpe on the north, and Abyla on the south side of the straits. But for more than two thousand years before this diversion of the name, the form of the material symbol was two pillars of wood or stone.

But how came the two pillars to be symbolized in the dollar-mark, and what was their original meaning?

The transfer of the title Pillars of Hercules to the two mountains furnishes at least a local beginning point in the answer to the first of these queries.

According to tradition, Melcarthus, a Tyrian navigator and explorer, sailing in search of fabled Atlantis or dimly rumored Britain, had paused in a bay at the western extremity of the land beyond the straits, and set up there two pillars as a memorial, building over them the temple of Hercules. A colony of Tyre was established there, and the place grew into the ancient Gades, the modern Cadiz. As the temple increased in wealth through the votive offerings of passing voyagers it became more splendid, and the first rude pillars of stone were replaced by others made of precious metals. As late as the second century this temple existed in its greatest splendor. Flavius Philostratus, who visited it, testifies to its magnificence, and in his Life of Apollonius of Tyana gives the following description of the pillars: —

"The pillars in the temple were composed of gold and silver, and so nicely blended were the metals as to form but one color. They were more than a cubit high, of a quadrangular form, like anvils, whose capitals were inscribed with characters neither Indian nor Egyptian, nor such as could be deciphered. *These pillars are the chain* which bind together the earth and* sea. The inscriptions on them were executed by Hercules in the house of the Parcte, to prevent discord arising among the elements and that friendship being disturbed which they have for each other."

These pillars were the nucleus of the ancient Gades, and naturally became the metropolitan emblem of the modern city, as the horse's head was of Carthage.

Leaving for the present the explanation of the original signification of the two pillars, the story of their descent to us may be briefly outlined as follows : —

When Charles V. became Emperor of Germany he adopted a new coat of imperial arms, in which those of Spain were quartered with those of the empire, the pillars of the arms of Cadiz being made supporters in the device.

At Seville was an imperial mint in which was coined a standard dollar called in the Mediterranean coasts "colonnato," the most prominent figures in the device on this coin being the two pillars and the scroll twined about them, the representation of which with a pen came to be the accepted symbol of the coin.

Melcarthus was a Tyrian, and the pillars must, therefore, have been known and reverenced as a sacred symbol in Tyre long before he set them up on the shores of the Atlantic. Additional proof of this may be found in the fact that on the coins of Tyre were prominently depicted, with some other emblems, two short pillars, arranged as supporters, one on either side of the general device, the proportions corresponding nearly to those described by Philostratus. The Tyrians, though not the first people to coin money, were the first to give it general circulation. Their coinage became the currency of the world, and the two pillars with which it was stamped would naturally become the symbol for money, so that the adoption of the dollar-mark to designate the "pillar pieces" of Charles V. was probably only the revival of an ancient custom which at first referred to the "pillar-pieces" of Tyre.

The pound-mark, £, in all probability owes its distinguishing feature, the two horizontal bars, to the same symbol, though in this connection they came into England by another route than Spain. The L was the initial letter of the Latin *Libra,* a balance, and was used to signify a standard by which to weigh the precious metals, the name of the weight being derived from the Roman *pondo,* a pound. But in the time of Henry VIII. the pound sterling which had been used as a standard for money was superseded by another pound, which had been brought from Cairo in Egypt to Troyes in France during the Crusades. In the two hundred years from the eleventh to the close of the thirteenth century, the zeal to recapture Jerusalem brought the people of Europe more in contact with each other, producing an interchange of ideas and customs, though the jealousies of the two or three most powerful nations retarded their general adoption. It was probably owing to the ancient hatred of Briton and Gaul that this Troyes weight was not definitely adopted in England until it was carried there by Venetian goldsmiths, about the year 1496. When it was so adopted it was probably distinguished from the old sterling, or "easterling" pound by adding to the pound-mark L two strokes of the pen to represent the pillars of Hercules, the common money symbol in the Mediterranean cities. But as the lower arm of the L was the shortest, a symmetrical written character could be made more easily by changing the pillars from the perpendicular to the horizontal. In handwriting, it is natural to make all straight marks slanting and not upright, and the change from slanting marks to horizontal ones would be as readily adopted as any other change in the symbol.

So much for the story of the two pillars as connected with money.

The tradition of the Freemasons in regard to the two pillars, which are a prominent emblem of their craft, is, that they represent the pillars *Jachin* and *Boaz* which Hiram of Tyre made for Solomon and set one on either side of the entrance to the Temple, to commemorate the pillar of cloud by day and of fire by night which guided the Israelites in their forty years' wanderings in the wilderness. Whatever significance the Hebrews may have attached to these pillars, there is good reason for believing that they received the material emblem from the Tyrians at the time of the building of the Temple. The Scriptures give a minute account of the dimensions and designs of the pillars (2 Kings vii., and 2 Chronicles iii.), but are silent as to their significance; and there is nothing in the whole Scriptural account of them to forbid the conclusion that the ideas symbolized by them were as much Tyrian as Jewish. Tyre had been a rich and prosperous city for over two hundred years when Solomon undertook the building of the Temple. The Tyrians had been skilled in architecture and other arts to a degree that implied a high state of mental culture while the Hebrews were yet nomadic tribes living in tents. The tabernacle was only a tent, and in this first Hebrew endeavor to give it a more enduring structure of wood and stone, Solomon naturally appealed to the greater skill of the subjects of the friendly Hiram, king of Tyre. When the Hebrews began to build the Temple they ceased their wanderings, they became permanently established, and, as a memorial of this fact, they embodied in the architectural design of the Temple a symbol which, by the Tyrians and many other nations descended from the ancient Aryan stock, was considered emblematic of a divine leadership that had conducted them to a new and permanent home; this was the true significance of the two pillars.

As long as the Hebrews were wander, erg the pillars of cloud by day and of fire by night were merely a metaphor, to express their belief in a divine direction of their movements. When they came at last to the promised land, the figurative pillars of cloud and fire became the two pillars in the porch of the Temple as the symbol of the establishment of the nation.

Having thus traced the story of the emblems back

through two lines of descent to a common point in Tyre, we must take a look into the remoter past to find the origin of the symbol in the earliest recorded ideas of the human race in connection with the Deity, and from that point we may follow its descent again through the two independent routes of Greek and Scandinavian mythology.

The ancient Aryans who composed the Vedas had not then arrived at the stage of intellectual development in which they could entertain the idea of an abstract principle as the one universal law, or of any god except a visible one. To them it seemed impossible that there could be a spiritual essence without some material form. Fire, the most inexplicable and striking of the agencies of nature, was accepted by them as this first and all-pervading force which controlled the universe; and the sun, the grandest and most brilliant mass of fire, as the embodiment of the Deity.

Here are two verses of the Vedas, as translated by Max Muller, which may be called the Genesis of the Brahmins, and in them are two words around which have crystallized fancies growing into myths, and myths growing into monuments of wood and stone, and again into ideal beings, until the original conceptions have been almost lost. Yet through all these changes some characteristics of the original meaning have been so stamped upon each new form, that the thread of connection, from those ancient days when the first peoples of the human race worshipped the sun on the plains of Central Asia, down through all the ages to the comparatively modern symbol of the Pillars of Hercules, is unmistakable: —

1. "In the beginning there arose the golden Child. He

was one born lord of all that is. He established the earth and this sky ; — Who is the God to whom we shall offer our sacrifice?

2. "He who gives life, he who gives strength, whose command all the bright gods revere, whose shadow is immortality; whose shadow is death ; — Who is the God to whom we shall offer our sacrifice?"

If there were nothing but the coincidence of the two words italicized in the foregoing verses, with the names of the two pillars in Solomon's Temple, — Jachin meaning strength, and Boaz *to establish,* — if there were nothing but this to establish the connection of the two pillars as well as the Pillars of Hercules and also the Greek myth of Castor and Pollux, with these ancient expressions, the identity of all these myths and symbols might be more doubtful than it is; but there is more.

In the Vedas the sun is called the "runner," the "quick racer"; he is called Arvat, the horse; Agni, the fire; Arusha, the red one, the strong one, the son of Heaven and Earth; Indra, the god of all gods. He is represented as drawn in a chariot over his daily course through the heavens by "the harits," "the rohits," and "the arushas," i.e. the gleaming, the ruddy, and the gold-colored horses of the dawn, which are the first rays of the morning sun.

The flexibility of the idea, within a certain range of expressions, seems to be acknowledged by the poets of the Vedas in the following verse : —

"Hear thou, the brilliant Agni, my prayer, whether the

two black horses bring thy car, or the two ruddy, or the two red horses."

Notwithstanding all the interchanging of names, numbers, and genders, and the changing of forms from animal to human and *vice versa,* there is an adherence to the idea of beings endowed with supernatural strength and brightness, and of a contest between, and alternating supremacy of, light and darkness!

It requires no great stretch of the imagination to conceive how, in the Greek modification of this many-sided plastic myth of the sun-god, Indra should be the prototype of Jove, and Arusha of Apollo, and also of Heracles. Indeed, it seems probable that, out of the numerous names of this one object of adoration, the sun, grew nearly all the wonderful and fantastic system of both Greek and Scandinavian mythology.

In the Vedic myths the phenomena which attended the rising and setting of the sun, the clouds, some black, some ruddy, and some shining like molten gold or silver, and also his first and last beams darting through, were spoken of as horses or cattle, or beings with human forms, almost invariably in *pairs.*

In some places the ruddy clouds that precede his rising are called the "bright cows." The two horses which the sun is said to harness to his car are called the "Arusha," the red ones; in other places they are called the "two Asvins," the shining mares; and in others the idea is modified still more, and they are called the "two sisters," and, at last, we find, are named Day and Night, the "daughters of Arusha," the one gleaming with the brightness of her father, and the other decked with stars. Professor Whitney, in his Essay on the Vedas, introduces the "two Asvins" as "enigmatical divinities," whose vocation or province in Aryan mythology he does not discover, though, at the same time, he intimates the probability that they may be identical with the Dioscuri of the Greeks; and Professor Miller hints at the same identity, but with no more reference to their true character of divine forerunners or guides for families, tribes, or races of men wandering about the world in search of new homes. It is related of the Dioscuri, that, when Castor was killed, Pollux, inconsolable for his loss, besought Jove to let him give his own life for that of his brother. To this Jove so far consented as to allow the two brothers to each pass alternate days under the earth and in the celestial abodes, their alternate daily deaths and ascensions into the heavens being only another version of the story of Day and Night, the daughters of Arusha. The twin brothers Castor and Pollux are represented as always clad in shining armor, and mounted on snow-white steeds, thus reproducing the chief characteristics of the "two Asvins," the shining mares of the Vedas, and showing that all these metamorphoses are only variations of the same idea.

The Hebrew metaphor of the pillar of cloud by day and of fire by night, to express the idea of a divine leadership, points to the same natural objects—clouds and fire — that to the earlier Aryans were symbols of the presence of the Deity; and the whole idea might seem a reproduction or elaboration of that expressed in the following verses of the Rig-Veda, written a thousand years before: —

"Wherever the mighty water - *cloud* vent, where they placed the seed and lit the *fire,* thence arose He who is the sole life of the bright gods; —Who is the God to whom we shall offer our sacrifice?

"He who by His might looked even over the water-clouds, the clouds which gave strength and lit the sacrifice; He who alone is God above all gods."

The fact that nearly every manifestation of the presence of the Deity recorded in Hebrew history down to the time of the building of the Temple was in a *cloud,* shows at least a remarkable resemblance to the Aryan conceptions of the divine presence.

The further elaboration of the idea in symbolizing the presence of the Deity by two pillars of wood or stone, and particularly of such presence in the character of a leader through long wanderings to a place of permanent establishment, was not exclusive with the Hebrews. Other races with whom the Hebrews could not have come in contact had precisely the same symbol of two pillars of wood or stone,—a fact which makes it a reasonable presumption that the two pillars, one of cloud one of fire, which were their prototypes, were not more exclusively a Hebrew idea.

In Sparta the twin Dioscuri are said to have been represented by two pillars of stone, which were sometimes joined by a smaller horizontal bar to represent their twinship. Frequently the top of one of these posts was carved in the semblance of a human head. The Spartans may have borrowed the emblem from the Tynans; the fact that the ancient Northmen employed the two pillars to symbolize precisely the same ideas as those connected with them by the Hebrews and Greeks makes it quite as likely that the Spartans derived the symbol from the same original source as the Tyrians.

A column of stone was in fact a common symbol of the deity among many ancient nations. Venus was worshipped at Paphos under the form of a stone. Juno of the Thespians and Diana of the Icarius were worshipped under the same form. The most famous of the Syrian deities was El Gabal (the stone), a name to which is akin the modern Arabic *gebel,* a mountain, or a rock. The very name of Gibraltar, one of the mountains to which poetry has transferred the title of Pillars of Hercules, is from Gebel Tarik, the mountain, or the rock, of Tarik, one of the first Moors who set foot on the northern side of the straits, and after whom came those who established in Spain the brilliant and romantic empire of these successors of the ancient Phoenicians.

There is good ground for the presumption that Heracles of the Greeks was only another version of the myth of the Dioscuri. The Hebrews gave each of the pillars a name, though they received the emblem from the Tyrians, who employed them as the emblem of one deity; and as the Tyrians were earlier than the Greeks, this phase of the monotheistic significance of the pillars must have come down from the same ancient source as the myth of the Dioscuri.

With both Greeks and Tyrians " Heracles," transformed by the Latins into "Hercules," seemed to be a transferable honorary title. The proper name of the Tyrian Heracles was Melcarthus, whose mother was said to be Asteria, the starry heavens; while the proper name of the Greek Heracles was Alcseus, who was said to be the son of Jove by a mortal mother, Alcmena, as the Dioscuri were said to be the twin sons of Jove by a mortal mother, Leda. The Heracles of the Tyrians and the

Castor and Pollux of the Greeks were the patron deities of seamen and navigators, as well as of feats of strength and agility.

Turning now to the mythology of the Scandinavians, we find in the character of Thor one which corresponds in all these particulars. He was said to be the son of Odin, the eldest of the gods, by Jord (the earth). Not only do the stories of his feats of strength with his hammer correspond to those of Heracles with his club, but he was the patron deity of the early Norse navigators who were as daring as even the Phoenicians.

The "sacred columns" of the Norse mythology were two high wooden posts, or pillars, fashioned by hewing. These stood on either side of the "high seat" of the master of the household, and hence were called "the pillars of the high seat," and were a sort of household symbol of Thor. The upper end of one of the pillars being, like the Spartan symbol, carved in the semblance of a human head, the setting up of these pillars was the sign of the establishment of the household on that spot. When a Northman moved, no matter how far, he took his sacred pillars with him; and where these were set up, there was his home until he made a formal change of domicile by moving them to some new spot.

When the Northmen discovered Iceland and began to emigrate there the sacred pillars of each Norse family were thrown overboard when the ship came near the land, and on the nearest habitable spot to where they were cast ashore by the waves they were set up, by planting the ends in the ground, as a symbol of possession, being in some respect a formal act of "entry," having something of the same significance as the act of the emigrant in the Western States who has "staked out a claim."

When the pillars were set up the house was built around them, and, though the pillars and the domicile might be moved to new locations, the place where the pillars were first cast ashore always retained a peculiar significance and sacredness to the family. Thus it is related of Throd Hrappsson, that his pillars, when cast overboard, were carried away by the waves and currents and apparently lost. He settled, however, on the eastern side of Iceland, and had been living there ten or fifteen years when it was discovered that his pillars had been cast ashore on the western coast, upon which he straightway sold his estate and moved to the locality where his pillars had been found.

Many other instances of the casting of the sacred columns into the sea, in order that they might guide Northmen in their selection of homes in Iceland, are related in Rudolph Keyser's Religion of the Northmen. Of Erik the Red it is told, that having loaned his posts of honor (possibly as a pledge of some promise to be fulfilled) to another Icelander, he could not get them back, which gave occasion for a long feud, into which many other families were drawn, and many of the adherents of both parties were slain. "When the Norse chieftain Thorolf Mostrarskegg left Norway to settle in Iceland he tore down the temple of Thor over which he had presided, — in which he seemed to have some kind of proprietary right from having built it chiefly at his own expense for the use of the worshippers of Thor, —and took with him the most of the timber, together with the earth beneath the platform on which Thor's statue had been seated." When he came in view of Iceland the two sacred columns of the temple were thrown into the sea; and where these were cast on shore by the waves he called the place Thorsnes, and built the temple of Thor, placing the two sacred columns, one on either side, just within the doorway.

The incidents in which the two columns thus appear in the earliest history of the Norse people are, it is true, of modern date when compared with their appearance at the building of Solomon's Temple, or the erection of the Pillars of Hercules by Melcarthus, near the Straits of Gibraltar; but their later appearance in history as the " Pillars of Thor " does not argue that they were copied from the Pillars of Hercules, but only that written history or even chronology of any kind was not known in Scandinavia until a much later period than in Syria and Greece. The Germanic race, however, of which the Northmen were a branch, had its origin in the center of Asia near the Caspian Sea. From there they had brought the same traditions as the Syrians and Greeks; and the religious myths out of which the Greeks afterwards elaborated their fanciful system of mythology were by the Northmen, whose rude climate gave imagination a gloomier turn, fashioned into the more barbarous, grotesque, and sanguinary "Asa faith." The cosmogony of the Greeks and the Northmen corresponds so nearly as to leave no doubt of a common origin, and yet the details were so different as to show that for ages the ancient stories must have been handed down from one generation to another by people possessed of a vastly different degree of refinement and surrounded by a different aspect of nature.

The Asa faith was as ancient as the cosmogony of the Phoenicians and the Greeks, and the sacred columns of Thor were not an idea borrowed from the Pillars of Heracles, but an independent perpetuation of the same mystic symbol.

The facts that the two pillars were a sacred symbol in three ancient and contemporaneous religions, and that they occupied the same position and significance in the temples of Thor of the Scandinavians, Heracles of the Tyrians, and Jehovah of the Hebrews, help to confirm the theory of a common mythology as the foundation and the source of the ideas of all the later faiths. The fervid spirit of the Hebrews gave to their version of this and other ancient conceptions a diviner mold. As the solar ray of light, split up by the prism, yields three groups of rays, one of which carries with it the main portion of the heat, another the greater part of all the light, and another nearly all the actinic qualities, and each of these groups embracing two or more of the seven prismatic colors, so the rays of that ancient Aryan sun, the first and most natural emblem of the Deity, falling on the human mind, have been elaborated into a great variety of faiths, each carrying with it some of the divine light, but in other characteristics as different as the groups in the spectrum of the analyzed solar ray. With one race the predominant traits of religious thought are brilliant, but merely sentimental corruscations of poetic fancy; with another, cold, practical maxims of thrift; with another, the fervid, but somber enthusiasm, the zealous dogmatism that overturns empires.

But in all there is the acknowledgment that the regular alternation of day and night is the work of God, the phenomena indicating his presence to guide man around the habitable portions of the world.

"Sun and moon go in regular succession, that we may see Indra and believe," writes one of the poets of the Rig-Veda.

"The day is thine, the night also is thine: thou hast prepared the light and the sun," sings the poet of Israel.

The Pillars of Freemasonry

By William Harvey

The uninitiated of the outer world who enter the precincts of a Masonic Lodge, or casts his curious eye upon the Diploma of a Master Mason, cannot fail to notice the twin pillars that form so prominent a feature in the decoration of the one and in the design of the other. Doubtless he contents himself with the reflection that, as the fraternity is intimately identified with building construction, these pillars are fit and proper symbols of Freemasonry. And if he cares to enquire he will find that his reflection is quite in keeping with the teachings of the Craft.

Illustrations of Freemasonry furnish pillars of many designs - from the simple Doric to the richly-decorated Composite - all set down according to the whim of the artist. And it is safe to say that, in general, they bear little resemblance to the pillars that stood at what is conventionally called "the porch or entrance to King Solomon's Temple." Whatever order of Architecture the design may represent, the pillars, as a rule, support massive globes which, in the language that belongs to modern Freemasonry, are said to represent the terrestrial and celestial spheres, and which are invariably decorated with geographical and stellar maps. As a rule, the pillars are shewn as placed at either side of the entrance way, and forming part of the building, but this very probably is incorrect, as the general view of Bible students and archaeologists is that the pillars were structurally independent of the Temple porch, and stood free in front of it, most likely on plinths or bases. Such free-standing pillars were a notable feature of temples in Western Asia, according to the writings of Greek authors, whose statements are borne out by designs on contemporary coins. Further proof of a conclusive character so far as these particular columns are concerned was furnished by an ancient glass dish which was discovered at Rome in 1882, and which presented an illustration of Solomon's Temple with the pillars standing free from the building and flanking the porch in the manner indicated.

The pillars which were brass or bronze-most probably the latter-nay be regarded as the highest expression of the art of their author, Hiram, "the half-Tyrian copper worker, whom Solomon fetched from Tyre to do foundry work for him." The stranger, we are told in the seventh chapter of the First Book of Kings, was "filled with wisdom and understanding and cunning, to work all works in brass "; and additional information concerning his artistic abilities may be gleaned from the second chapter of the Second Book of Chronicles, where it is stated that he was "skillful to work in gold, and in silver, in brass, in iron, in stone, and in timber, in purple, in blue, and in fine linen, and in crimson." Building upon that foundation, Freemasons have not hesitated to claim him as "the principal Architect of the Temple," and have grouped his name with those of Hiram, King of Tyre, and Solomon, King of Israel, in a trinity of genius and piety.

The pillars are described in the seventh chapter of the

First Book of Kings, but scholars agree that the description is exceedingly confused and corrupt. By collating the references there, however, with allusions in other books of the Old Testament, students arrive at what they regard as a fairly accurate account of the columns. Accordingly they tell us that Hiram "cast the two pillars of bronze for the porch of the temple; 18 cubits was the height of the one pillar, and a line of 12 cubits could compass it about, and its thickness was 4 finger breadths (for it was) hollow. And the second pillar was similar. And he made two chapiters [i.e., capitals] of cast bronze for the tops of the pillars: the height of the one chapiter was 5 cubits, and the height of the other chapiter was 5 cubits. And he made two sets of network to cover the chapiters which were upon the tops of the pillars, a network for the one chapiter, and a network for the second chapiter. And he made the pomegranates; and two rows of pomegranates in bronze were upon the one network, and the pomegranates were 200, round about upon the one chapiter, and so he did for the second chapiter. And upon the top of the pillars was lily-work: so was the work of the pillars finished." It is interesting to compare this description with that preserved by Josephus, the Jewish historian. He writes that, "Hiram made two hollow pillars, whose outsides were of brass, and the thickness of the brass was four fingers' breadth, and the height of the pillars was eighteen cubits, and their circumference twelve cubits; but there was cast with each of their chapiters lily-work that stood upon the pillar, and it was elevated five cubits, round about which there was net-work, interwoven with small palms made of brass and covering the lilywork. To this also were hung two hundred pomegranates in two rows."

The pillars were cast in the plain of the Jordan, in the clay ground between Succoth and Zeredatha. This spot was about thirty-five miles north-east of Jerusalem, and the belief is that Hiram erected his foundry there on account of the fact that the clay which abounded in that locality was, by its great tenacity, peculiarly fitted for making molds. Authority for this view is found in the 42nd verse of the 7th chapter of the First Book of Kings, and in the 17th verse of the 4th chapter of the Second Book of Chronicles, and further confirmation of the Masonic tradition is supplied by Morris in his work on "Freemasonry in the Holy Land." He says that one of his assistants discovered that the jewelers of Jerusalem at the present day use a particular species of brown arenaceous clay in making molds for casting small pieces of brass. On his inquiring whence this clay came, he was informed that it was got at "Seikoot, about two-days' journey north-east of Jerusalem."

The metal was of a thickness equal to three inches of our measure, and, taking the larger cubit of 20½ inches as a standard, the pillars reached to a height of about 31 feet, while in diameter they were about 6½ feet.

The details of the pillars fall naturally into four parts-the columns, the lily work, the capitals or chapiters, and the ornamentation thereof. All authorities agree that the pillars were hollow, and a Masonic tradition - which, however, is generally regarded as a myth - alleges that they were so formed the better to serve as archives for the Craft, and that within them were deposited the constitutional rolls of the fraternity. At the junction of the pillar and the chapiter, and springing out from the former, was a row of lily petals which, according to one account, "first spreading round the chapiter, afterwards gently curved downwards towards the pillar, something like the acanthus leaves on the capital of a Corinthian column," and, Lightfoot gives a fuller description when he says, "at the head of the pillar, even at the setting on of the chapiter, there was a curious and a large border or circle of lily-work, which stood out four cubits under the chapiter, and then turned down, every lily or long tongue of brass, with a neat bending, and so seemed as a flowered crown to the head of the pillar, and as a curious garland whereon the chapiter had its seat."

The lily-work supported the chapiter with which each column was crowned. Reference has already been made to the fact that in Masonic illustrations the pillars are commonly represented as upholding spheres, and sometimes Freemasons teach that these globes "contained the maps and charts of the celestial and terrestrial bodies, denoting the universality of Masonry." All this is imagination. The capitals were not surmounted by spheres, but the capitals themselves appear from the reference in the seventh chapter of the First Book of Kings to have been globular or spheroidal in form. Lightfoot says the capital "was a huge, great oval . . . and did not only sit upon the head of the pillars, but also flowered or spread them, being large about, a great deal, than the pillars themselves." These capitals added 82 feet to the height of the columns, and thus the complete pillars rose to an altitude of roughly 40 feet.

67

The capitals were richly decorated, and the ornamentation was of a twofold character. About two-fifths of the distance from the bottom, or just below the most bulging part of the globular chapiter, a tissue of net-work was carved, which extended over its whole upper surface. To the bottom of this net-work was suspended a series of fringes, and these again were festooned with two wreaths of bronze pomegranates. We gather from what is said in the 52nd chapter of Jeremiah that four of the pomegranates were fixed to the net-work and that the remaining ninety-six hung free.

Authorities are not agreed as to the purpose of these pillars. One view set forth-and it is regarded as entirely improbable by those who differ from it is that the pillars were huge candelabra or cressets in which "the suet of the sacrifices" was burned. Another view is that the pillars can be explained in terms of the astral mythology of Babylon. A third suggestion is that, as they were the work of a Phoenician artist, their meaning should be sought for by a reference to the similar pillars that were to be found in Phoenician temples. In this connection it is interesting to note that, according to Herodotus, the temple at Tyre, with which Hiram must have been familiar, contained two such pillars, one of emerald, and the other of fine gold. In primitive times pillars had been regarded as the abode of the Deity, and probably the standing stones all the world over are to be explained in some such way. As civilization advanced, however, the pillar ceased to become the abode but continued to be a symbol of the presence of God. It is not unlikely that Hiram, imbued with the religious beliefs of his native land, gave the pillars a place in his plan as conventional symbols of the God for whose worship the Temple of Solomon was designed.

Freemasons teach that the pillars were set up by the wise King as a memorial to the Children of Israel of the happy deliverance of their forefathers from their Egyptian bondage, and in commemoration of the Pillars of Fire and Cloud, which had two wonderful effects-the fire gave light to the Israelites during their escape from their Egyptian bondage; the cloud proved darkness to Pharaoh and his followers when they attempted to overtake the Hebrews. Such an event in the history of the race deserved ever to be kept before the eyes of the Jewish people, and Freemasons maintain that it was with this object in view that the Pillars were set up at the entrance to the Temple, since that was the most proper and conspicuous situation in which they might be observed by those who attended the ordinances of divine worship. It is thus seen that the teachings of the Craft are not out of harmony with the views attributed to Hiram. It is suggested that the Phoenician artist raised the pillars as symbols of Divine Majesty; the Freemason regards them as memorials of the manifestations of Divine Providence as seen in the Pillars of Fire and Cloud.

We read in the seventh chapter of the First Book of Kings and again in the third chapter of the Second Book of Chronicles, that Hiram "set up the right pillar and called the name thereof Jachin; and he set up the left pillar, and called the name thereof Boaz." Why the pillars were so named remains one of the mysteries of Biblical antiquities; but Freemasonry has its own explanations. We learn from the seventeenth verse of the 24th chapter of the First Book of Chronicles that Jachin was the head of the twenty-first division of priests in the time of David, and Freemasonry says that the Pillar was named after Jachin, the assistant high priest who officiated at the dedication of the Temple. Boaz took its name from Boaz, the great-grandfather of King David. By some rabbis this Boaz is identified with the judge Ibzan of Bethlehem who is mentioned in the eighth verse of the twelfth chapter of judges; and according to Jewish tradition he was the father of sixty children, all of whom died during his lifetime because he did not invite Manoah, Samson's father, to any of the marriage festivities in his house. Late in life he became the hero of the idyll of the harvest field in which Ruth the Moabitess figured. Boaz was eighty years of age when he married Ruth, who was forty. He died the day after the wedding, but the marriage did not remain childless. Ruth bore a son whose name was Obed, and who, according to the Old Testament, was the grandfather of David. Modern critics generally deny the historical value of the genealogy, but Masons accept the statement, and the controversy may safely be left as a nut for antiquaries to crack.

Our English Bible, in its marginal references, suggests renderings of the names of the Pillars, interpreting Jachin as meaning "he shall establish," and Boaz as meaning "in its strength." Bible students agree that these readings are very problematical, and give no help to a proper understanding of why the Pillars were so named. Freemasonry, incorporating them into its symbolic teaching, says that the two, when conjoined, refer to the stable or enduring quality of all things that belong to the eternal God, fortifying the whole with the phrase, "For God said, 'In Strength will I establish this mine house that it may stand forever.'" And there cannot be any doubt but that pillars of such magnitude could not fail to impress the minds of those who beheld them, alike by their massive proportions, their strength, and their beauty.

As symbols of these qualities they should still be potent with meaning for Freemasons.

The Network upon the capitals is emblematical of that Unity which should at all times characterize members of the Craft. As one mesh of the net is interwoven with another, so the threads of all our lives intertwine. No man liveth unto himself; and it is the duty of a brother to recognize the mutual responsibilities of life by extending help to those who are in need, sympathy to those who are in affliction, and counsel to those who depend upon him for guidance.

The Lilywork denotes Peace and Purity. The white lily is one of the flowers of the fields of Judea, and there are frequent references to it in the Bible as an emblem of purity. It was full of meaning to the ancients, and occurs all over the East; and indeed has been held in mysterious veneration by people of all nations and times. In the arms of France the three leaves of the lily mean Piety, Justice, and Charity, a trinity of characteristics that cannot fail to command the esteem of all good Masons. As a symbol of Purity it reminds us of that purity of life and action which should at all times distinguish us if we would be true to the tenets of our moral code. As a symbol of Peace, it denotes that Peace which, whether in the home, in the Lodge, or in the State, is best promoted by a faithful observance of the rights of others. Only thus may discord be banished from the home, enmity debarred from the Lodge, and war prevented from exciting the jealousies of nations and provoking men to massacre.

The Pomegranate from the exuberance of its seeds denotes Plenty. As an emblem it was highly esteemed by the nations of antiquity who attached some mystic signification to its fruit. It is believed to have been worshiped as a god by the Syrians of Damascus, and there was a temple on Mount Cassius (between Canaan and Egypt) in which there was an image of Jupiter with a pomegranate in his hand. To the modern Freemason it denotes that Plenty which is the fruit of a wise exercise of the gifts with which we have been endowed, and which, devoted with a single eye to the advancement of civilization, may enable each of us to enter at last into the Eternal Silence, conscious that we have done what we could to raise mankind to a higher plane of moral and social life.

The conjoined names of the Pillars denote Stability - that stability of character and of purpose which should ever be apparent in the life of the Freemason who would stand fast in the faith. He must be stable in friendship, only thus may he enjoy and promote the privileges of brotherhood. He must be stable to withstand the assaults of evil, otherwise his character may be tarnished and his whole life laid in ruins. He must be stable in the defense of truth and honor so that men, seeing him and testing him, may learn what Freemasonry is, and what are the great principles for which our system stands.

Someone has said that a Freemason's lodge is the universe, and that Jachin and Boaz are the two pillars that support and sustain it. It is a happy conceit, and from it one might argue that every Freemason is a pillar in the great temple of universal brotherhood. And, just as the strength of a chain is measured by its weakest link, so the stability of the Temple, is tested by the strength of the pillars which support it. Therefore, each craftsman should strive constantly to cultivate the wisdom of understanding a brother's wants, the strength of aiding a brother to bear the burden of life, and the beauty of a timely and discerning benevolence.

In all ages, pillars have occupied a prominent place in the life and thought of nations. Heredotus tells us that the Egyptians erected their obelisks in honor of the sun, and that their pointed form was intended to represent his rays. Jacob set up a pillar at Bethel to memorialize his vision of the ladder that reached from earth to heaven; Joshua raised twelve pillars at Gilgal to perpetuate the memory of his miraculous crossing of the Jordan; Samuel erected a pillar between Mizpeh and Shem to record the defeat of the Philistines; and Absolom reared one in honor of himself. The Hebrews regarded them, too, as symbols of princes and nobles who were the pillars of the state. Thus, in the third verse of the eleventh Psalm, the passage which in our translation reads, "If the foundations be destroyed," is, in the original, "When the columns are overthrown," that is, when the firm supports of what is right and good have perished, "what can the righteous do?" Again, the tenth verse of the nineteenth chapter of Isaiah should, more accurately be rendered, "Her (Egypt's) columns are broken down," that is, the nobles of her State have been overthrown. And many other instances might be cited.

The rude standing-stone on the lonely moor, and the richly-sculptured column in the teeming city-square are alike emblems of a people's faith. In a thousand God's acres you will find a broken column raised as a memorial of a young life that has been cut short by the grim tyler of Eternity. Pillars are set up to mark the resting places of kings, the spots where nations have contended for freedom, and in the centers of civic life where law and order are proclaimed. Each is an index finger of thought pointing the meditative man to the record of a steadily advancing civilization. Pillars, too - - the expression of an altruistic faith - - are set up on every inhabited shore washed by the waters of the world to guide the mariner from the rocks and reefs that lure him to destruction.

And as all are raised by the mallet and chisel of the operative, so all may be eloquent with singularly wise speech for the speculative Mason. The standing stone, though but the emblem of a pagan faith, bears witness to the eternal belief in God; the monument in the city square embodies a nation's desire that the memory of great men shall not die; the pillar that marks the resting place of Kings, or the spot where freedom has been won, or the laws of government have been proclaimed, is the symbol of a people's loyalty, and the expression of the universal sense of justice and right.

Yet while all these-belief in God, honor to men, loyalty to the King, and recognition of social rights-are tenets of our

Masonic faith, perhaps in a truer sense is the Pillar that guides the lonely mariner at sea a symbol of our Craft. What is Freemasonry if it is not a giant lighthouse? Down through the years its kindly beams have shone across the troubled waters of life, carrying with them their message of hope and goodwill and kindly thought for those in peril and distress. And it is not too much to assert that, just as the Pillar or Cloud by day and the Pillar of Fire by night, led and protected the fathers of Solomon in their dreary march from the land of bondage to the house of freedom, so the twin pillars, whose names are Jachin and Boaz, have been the means of bringing happiness and joy into the hearts of countless thousands of our race.

www.ingramcontent.com/pod-product-compliance
Lightning Source LLC
LaVergne TN
LVHW041457070426
835507LV00009B/656